Facing Cancer

Also by Brenda Eldridge and published by Ginninderra Press

Poetry
The Silver Cord
It's All Good
A Personal View
Facing Cancer
From My Garden
Best Heard & Seen
Scarves
Tangled Roots: new & selected poems
Elemental (Pocket Poets)
Forgotten Dreams (Pocket Poets)
Wonderment

Non-fiction
Down by the River
Tales From My Patagonia
It's Still Out There
There's a Rainbow Serpent In My Garden
Eastwards
From Patagonia to Australia
Forty Green (Pocket Places)
Who Was She? (Pocket People)
Dear Dad (Pocket People)

Edited by Brenda Eldridge and published by Ginninderra Press
Brave Enough To Be a Poet
The Heart of Port Adelaide
Collecting Writers

Brenda Eldridge

Facing Cancer

Acknowledgement

An earlier version of the introduction to *Facing Cancer* was first published in *Voice* Issue 36, under the title Hurry Up and Wait

To Annette, Joan and Zenda

Facing Cancer
ISBN 978 1 74027 661 0
Copyright © text Brenda Eldridge 2011

First published 2011
Reprinted 2016

GINNINDERRA PRESS
PO Box 3461 Port Adelaide SA 5015
www.ginninderrapress.com.au

Contents

When Cancer Came to Call	7
Race For Life	15
Thoughts Against the Dark	17
Not Just Another Day	18
Glorious Life	19
Drooping Roses	20
The Sound of Hope	21
Dark Corridors	22
Comfortable Silence	23
Routines	24
Power of Words	26
Doubt Dragon	28
Shock Waves	30
Shelter From the Storm	32
Wordsmiths Silenced	34
Aftermath	36
Cancer	37
Dark Shadow	39
Going Home	40
Reprieve	42
Celebration Bash	44
Going On	45
Trust	46
Return Visits	48
Paradox	50
Five Minutes a Day	51
Not Vanity	52
Delusion of Next Door	53
Reminder	54
Time Out	56

Life	58
Another Reality	59
Half-kisses	60
In Awe	61
Dungeon	62
Tree Help	63
Metallica	65
No Claustrophobia Today	66
Natural Remedies	67
Identification	69
A Little Harmless Deception	71
Only Lunch	72
Time Passing	73
Walk a Mile In His Shoes	74
Courage Is Hard To Measure	75
Passionate Alternative	76
No More Questions	78
Necessity	80
Almost Done	82
Old Tricks	84
Ducks and Swans	85
Bereft	86
Last Day	88
Living	89
The Outer Edge	91

When Cancer Came to Call

Towards the end of 2010 I often found myself quoting Robert Burns: 'The best laid plans of mice and men…' It perfectly sums up what our life was like then. We were merrily going along, grateful that life was so good. Then without warning our life exploded into thousands of pieces because of one word – 'cancer'.

The moral of this story is 'If you have an ulcer in your mouth that your dentist dismisses, and it doesn't go away quickly – find a new dentist.' We did, and in a matter of three days we were seeing a specialist and were on an amazing roller coaster that resembled a race for life. The gargantuan public hospital system included us in its trundling, rumbling passage through people's lives with militaristic precision, and the mottos of 'hurry up and wait' and 'prepare for the worst and hope for the best' were to the forefront.

This is not a horror story – there are far too many of those around. No, ours is a story of a serendipitous string of events, and the right people being in the right place at the right time.

After some preliminary scans, we were invited to a meeting of about fifteen surgeons and specialists who gathered to discuss the best course of action. We were blessed with four highly respected specialists and surgeons who proved to be humanitarians as well. The simple gesture of a hand on Stephen's shoulder did more to quiet fear and panic than endless words could have done. At each appointment, while we were being drip-fed more and more unpalatable information, these men extended their compassion to me. Not once was I made to feel foolish because of my ignorance and simple questions.

I did question a doctor about the drip-feed process and he agreed that they have to do it that way. Statistics show that as soon as the word 'cancer' is mentioned people stop listening properly, and at each consultation retain only about twenty per cent of information. At each session, to overcome this, everything is repeated from the beginning and then something new is added at the end. I have to say that we went into shock at the first mention of cancer, and in many ways we are still there.

Entering into this arena, there comes a time when you must make a conscious decision to trust that the doctors will do their very best. This was hard for Stephen because he is a self-confessed control-freak, and to place himself in the doctors' hands took a lot of courage. The decision to trust also helped when we came up against the drip-feed process. In the beginning Stephen was told only two teeth needed to be removed and then it would be all over. This was gradually increased over a few visits to being told that five teeth would need to be extracted. Then we were being told, 'The cancer may have spread into the jaw, so a piece of bone will have to be taken from your hip and a jaw reconstruction done. Oh, and while there's no evidence to indicate that the cancer has spread to your lymph system, but just to be sure, as a precaution, we'll remove the lymph glands on that side of your neck.' Next it was 'Well, there are all these nerves running around from the back of your ear to your throat. Theoretically, they're in the same place for everyone but this is never a certainty and if one or some of them get damaged – well, you could end up not being able to shrug your shoulders.' Then 'With regard to the nerves connected to the corner in your mouth – it may mean your mouth will probably droop a little and you may dribble a bit – and part of the bottom lip will be a bit numb. Because the cancer's heading towards your tongue, well, there may be some residual eating difficulty and speech impairment. Now, because we're working at the back of your jaw there will be swelling, which could impede your breathing, so you'll have a temporary tracheostomy as a precaution. There'll be swelling on the inside of your mouth which will go down in a few weeks.'

I'm not sure if or when we paused for breath when we were being presented with all that information, but I'm sure you're beginning to get the picture about that decision to trust.

Only four weeks after the initial diagnosis, Stephen was admitted for surgery. It took this team of incredibly talented people nine hours to complete the job. That for Stephen was the easiest part – after all, he was asleep. But the next twelve days and nights were horrendous for Stephen, as he is a very private man. A man of quiet dignity and great sensitivity, he was thrust unwittingly into a world where nothing was sacred. We learned the true value of black humour and grim determination.

There are strange rewards for doing well in hospital. The three days he was expected to be in the intensive care unit turned out to be less than twenty-four hours. His period of stay in a one-bed room was quickly reduced and he was moved to a six-bed ward. His bed was at the end near the window, and while his only view was the tall building opposite, there was some degree of privacy, if we pulled the curtains around.

Anyone who has suffered the indignity of being fed by nasal drip will understand Stephens's horror at the tube being put in place immediately before leaving ICU. Stephen had no idea how appalling and restrictive it was going to be to have a disgusting mixture poured into him for two hours, every four hours. It may have contained everything Stephen needed from a nutritional point of view, but that didn't help much.

Looking back, the nutritionist's attitude was one of the few negatives in a very difficult situation. She no doubt knew her theory well, but she must have fallen asleep at the lecture on listening to the concerns or needs of the patients she was attending. Stephen recognised he was talking to a brick wall and let her do what she wanted to. It was all about ticking the right boxes so that he could get home. However, on the quiet he did mutter and snarl about her a lot, and to all and sundry since. Perhaps she has become the focus for other frustrations.

The magic day arrived when he was allowed a drink of water from a glass. His toes curled in pleasure. Straight after that a small tub of fruit appeared. I watched enchanted to see a man delight in this simplest of pleasures – real food ingested in an ordinary way!

For the first few days, the tracheostomy meant Stephen couldn't talk. We were reduced to pen and paper and it was so frustrating for him to have to write things down and find he wasn't always understood. One of the surgeons eventually came and made some adjustments to the tracheostomy, but neglected to tell Stephen that if he put his finger over the end, he could talk. It was a couple of hours later when one of our favourite nurses showed him how to do this. Ah, such freedom.

When the drainage tubes were removed from his neck and hip, and the catheter was taken out, Stephen was free to learn how to walk. A mystery was solved. While in his little room we had heard a frequent squeaking noise – much like a child wailing – and we couldn't work out what it was. When they gave Stephen a walking frame, we found out what it was. The heavier it was leaned on, the louder it squeaked.

But the walking frame was Stephen's path to freedom. I have never witnessed such determination. Every possible moment, he was pacing the corridors. We must have walked miles – well, it certainly felt like it – setting new goals every time one was achieved. We became this funny old couple out strolling through different places in the world, our imaginations taking us all over the place. But it worked. Quickly Stephen started walking with more confidence. His progress was reflected in his attitude to everything as he 'walked off' the tag of invalid. The physiotherapist was stunned to meet us out in the corridor one day, and instantly stated that the frame was a hindrance, not a help, and provided him with a walking stick.

I am certain that one of the essential keys not only to a good recovery, but to getting the best out of nursing staff and everyone else connected to the healing process, is to be cooperative. The hospital used the term 'compliant patient'. They quickly knew that Stephen was going to do everything possible to get home. He was always cheerful, helpful and polite – simply being who he naturally is, and this was rewarded with these courtesies being returned to him.

It was inevitable that there were seriously dark times too. Like his first night out of ICU when he had one-to-one nursing. He was in distress coughing and rang for the nurse and she didn't come. He felt utterly abandoned, unable to breathe properly and unable to call for help. His mind reacted to the vast amounts of anaesthetic they had poured into him for the surgery, and every time he closed his eyes he experienced alarming hallucinations. He was afraid to sleep, but gradually this wore off. During those darkest hours he reached an all-time low and wanted to rip out all the tubes and devices, and put an end to it all. Words cannot describe the terrible place he found himself in and if you have been there, words are not needed.

On the twelfth day, Stephen was allowed to come home, but not before the doctors fired two passing shots – 'radiotherapy' and 'chemotherapy'. In my ignorance I put two and two together and decided that the surgery hadn't got the cancer and started to panic. It turned out that the margins were narrow and the radiotherapy was a precaution. The tests came back showing that there was no evidence of cancer in the bone. So, yes we can breathe a little easier now.

Stephen started radiotherapy treatment three days ago. He has to have thirty sessions that will finish just before Christmas. They tell us his face will look and feel as if it is sunburnt, the inside of his mouth will blister, which will make eating difficult, and he will get very tired. Horrible to contemplate, but still we are aware that this is a small price to pay for life.

I have written of the 'action' aspects to this journey. I have not mentioned the extraordinary support we have been given. It seemed to help Stephen if I was at the hospital as much as possible. The twelve hours a day I spent with him were a pleasure. The hour travelling at each end of the day was not so good. It didn't take long for me to get over-tired, overwhelmed and over-everything. I was needlessly worried about the business and attempted to keep up with a lot of the business emails. The sleep fairy went AWOL about three o'clock in the morning, and two or three very dear friends received some very revealing emails. There were so many cards and emails coming in, people sending best wishes and love and, best of all, being mentioned in their prayers. Even now I cannot think about that support without weeping – for the best of reasons.

We went out for a meal last night with a friend. He too had experienced a brush with cancer, which fortunately was a false alarm. He said something that has enabled me to face my own fears and be able to write this article. He said that we have been able to find cures for most conditions that have caused early deaths in years gone by, and all that are left are the really nasty ones – like cancer. He said cancer has become the synonym for death. How shockingly accurate he is.

I can reflect on those words and more clearly understand why some people in our lives have been unable to face that. It is heart-breaking to witness the denial of a nasty reality, especially when that is what you want to do yourself. It is painful to experience the pretence of acting as if everything is back to normal now the surgery is over, knowing that 'normal' will never be quite the same again.

What about anger too? The 'why me?' question was answered by the doctors – 'just bad luck'. Stephen's cancer is one that usually comes from smoking and drinking heavily – neither of which he has ever done. I turned my fear into anger. That hasn't helped anyone, and gradually I am turning it into something positive, which I have done at other challenging times in my life, by writing poetry.

Stephen's life as the owner of Ginninderra Press is all about giving people access to experiences that they might not have themselves. He did not want to write this article – it is too close – but I believe it is too important a story not to be told. Cancer is every bit as scary as we imagined it would be and worse, but it has made us aware of how sweet the gift of life is. Our realisations have touched everyone connected to us and this has rippled into wider and wider circles. This is the heart of Ginninderra Press.

Brenda Eldridge

Race For Life

We seem to be like athletes
With all that build-up to bring us
To the starting blocks
And now here we sit in a waiting room
Just waiting for what comes next

We have no horror stories
About our experiences in the hospital
The staff without exception
Have treated us with kindness and respect
But never the less, the race is just starting

I don't remember anyone telling me
About this thing called
The race for life
I thought we plodded along
Enjoying the world around us

Making the best of every day
Trying not to hurt anyone
Jumping the occasional hurdles
Falling flat on our faces
Limping along at times

Even wondering vaguely
How long the journey would be
Being shocked to the core
When some lives were so short
Suddenly it's like being in a military unit

Where life is so much
'Hurry up…and wait'
'Prepare for the worst
And hope for the best'
We would rather be watching the dolphins

Thoughts Against the Dark

The river is a blazing shimmering dance of light
Sparkles flash like diamonds
The sun is reflecting rainbow colours
From the crystal star hanging in the window
I am surrounded by brilliance

In a life rich with love
I have not experienced since childhood
This sense of safety and awaiting promise
I have no secret longings or unfulfilled dreams
I do not need to prove myself

I won't try and make bargains with the gods
They know my journey they know my heart
I won't wish precious time away
To hurry knowing an outcome
I will savour each moment here in the light

Knowing that this feeling
Will be with me for the rest of my life
A quiet certainty in the depths
That I will always be surrounded by light
And lit from within by a steadfast love

Not Just Another Day

All afternoon and evening we sat in the hospital
The day before your surgery
You kept us doing cryptic crosswords
It was good to meet the anaesthetist
I loved his quiet self-assurance

It was he who said it was alright
For me to come at seven in the morning
To walk with you to the theatre
You were laughing with the nurses
When I left you at eight-fifty

I was mindless all day
It was my choice to be alone
I know I started preparing two paintings
There is always a time for favourite movies
And Harry Potter and Tolkien worked their magic

Six twenty-five the call came
Nine hours of surgery
But you had come through
Sleeping peacefully in ICU
Now all we had to do was wait

I sent text messages and e-mails
To immediate family
To share not just the news
But the relief you were all right
How little idea I had of the journey ahead

Glorious Life

Breakfast out on the balcony
The freshness of the air on my skin
The stillness of the reach
Are smoothing away the jitters
That robbed me of sleep in the midnight hours

My favourite dolphin cruised by
So close I could almost touch him
Some tears shed are so healing
There are pelicans as usual on the posts
And cormorants diving for breakfast

Seagulls and sparrows make a strange choir
As do swallows and parakeets
The jasmine is sensuously sweet
My second cup of tea is cold
And come to think of it so are my feet

But how rich I am
Life threw an unexpected challenge
That I do not have to fight alone
Such an outpouring of love and prayers
Has held me safe from despairing

Two women are rowing past
What a lovely sound the oars make
A train is squealing round the bend
The crossing bells are clanking
Oh glorious life continuing

Drooping Roses

I brought in the first rose of spring
It was only a fat bud
But I thought it would bring
The outdoors into this
Small and enforced place

I have had the little vase
For many years
It was a treat for myself
After Mark died
To hold a flower on my office desk

When I arrived this morning
The rose's head had drooped
And I refilled the vase with water
And very slowly it began to straighten
But it never did open

I feel like that rose
I was flourishing in the garden
With Stephen's steady hand
Learning to allow joy
To banish grief and angst

Suddenly I was plucked and thrust
Into a world of fear and panic
Drooping under the onslaught
But even from his hospital bed
I feel Stephen's strength

The Sound of Hope

Not for us the strains
Of perfectly harmonised notes
The soaring cadence of voices
Rejoicing in the joy of life
As written by a gifted composer

Or the sound of rain
Falling on a tin roof
Marking perhaps the beginning
Of the end of
Devastating drought

We listen intently
To the doppler
As it measures the strength
Of the blood flowing through
The veins after the bone graft

We hear that beautiful sound
And know a small release
Of the tension within
Yes the surgery is working
It is for us the sound of hope

Dark Corridors

Look into the eyes
Of someone who has spent
Time in hospital
With little warning
And less idea of what was happening

All freedoms gone
Where to be   When to be
What to wear   What to eat
Silence a gem of the past
Fresh air a distant memory

Permission given in a daze
'Yes, you may do these things to save my life'
While inside every vestige of their being
Is screaming in outraged denial
'How dare you assault me so'

The eyes tell the story
Of long long hours
Lying helpless in a bed
Forever jousting with demons
Real and imagined

Comfortable Silence

It has been a desire
For so many long years
To sit in comfortable silence
With one who is untroubled
By the lack of noise

We are trapped here in the hospital
Around us are the continuous
Background noises
Bangs and clatters of equipment
Sometimes a loud cry

In this room there is
The rushing sound of oxygen
A machine beeping
The soft rustle of a foot
Moving across the sheets

But we are at peace
He is reading a book
And resisting falling asleep
I sit here writing
It's like a river always flowing

We make our own haven
Wherever we are
Alert and attentive
To each other's needs
Nourished by this peace between us

Routines

There is great comfort
To be drawn from routine
How quickly a pattern formed
That I could rely on
That kept me stable

Seven forty-five leaving home
Emptying the post office box
Eight seventeen the train to town
A walk in early morning freshness
Along North Terrace to the hospital

You listened for my footsteps
Only relaxing when I appeared
At the end of your bed
Breathless from walking and anxious
To know that you were alright

Eight forty-five in the evening
The hospital settling for the night
I reluctantly had to leave
The shelter of being with you
And start my journey home

How frightened I was standing at the bus stop
Sending an SMS to Annette
To discourage anyone from approaching me
Trying not to panic if the bus was late
But also watching the waxing moon

I sat on the single seat
The closest to the driver
I pretended to read a book
Sometimes I even watched
The world go by

Then I had to get off the bus
And pray from heart and soul
To be kept safe
As I walked rapidly
Through the shopping centre car park

I was more scared if there were people about
Than the dark emptiness
I scampered home along familiar streets
Not relaxing till the garden gate locked behind me
Praying again my thanks

Power of Words

People talk a lot about the power of words
And if poets are involved
Our minds often drift
To romantic sonnets
Or odes to a something

A tracheostomy had robbed you of speech
And you were left to communicate
With pen and paper
Which meant the messages were brief
Cut right down to bare necessity

We had a routine by then
The first thing I did each morning
Was to text to your son how you were
And the words had been
Full of your positive progress

'Three sides of the tumour are clear
The fourth side not certain
I will not have another op
We will make the best of the time we have'
If there was more I can't remember now

I can be as strong as is needed
I can get by on little sleep
And still do what must be done
But there is always a price to pay
And I have my limits

I sent a text message
Changing only the first two lines to
They didn't get all the cancer
No doubt there was a better way
But hindsight is easy

Doubt Dragon

You couldn't help yourself could you?
Saw a window of opportunity
And you were in like Flynn
And all credit to you
You did a grand job – for a while

But I am wise to your tactics
You forget I've tamed you before
The first time you were called
The Why Road and you nearly got me
Took me to the edge of sanity too

The second time you were called Guilt
You certainly made me fight hard
Quick as a flash if I felt
The warmth of a smile in heart or mind
You hammered me back down

I turned you into a poem
I even used the F word
When I told you to go to hell in a basket
I didn't need you any more
And you are published

You came as Grief
That was the hardest of all
You almost succeeded in grinding
My love of life to dust
You cast such a long shadow

And in that guise
You are often sneaking around
Catching me off guard
With a piece of music
Or a familiar voice or laugh

Do you like your new name?
I thought Doubt Dragon
Acknowledged well your ferocity
You haven't changed much
Still an insidious monster

I have different strength now
Not as passionate and defiant
I have patience and quietude
A depth of love and support
You can't come close to destroying

So go your hardest, Dragon,
If you think I need reminding
That you will always be
The darkness that makes
The light so precious

Shock Waves

My mind is like a bowl of words
That I can dip my pen in
And they pour onto the empty page
Creating beautiful images
To delight a reader

But when a sudden shock
Falls from the great unknown
And lands in this bowl
The words are splattered
Over the edges and disappear

Then they slow to swirling around
Too slippery for my mind
To grasp with nerveless fingers
And string tidily together
To make sense of the carnage

Like a rat in a maze
Screaming silently
My mind exhausts itself running
Hither and thither through the darkness
Then the shuddering begins

How can I tell anyone
When I can't catch the words
To explain the slipping and sliding
At best I reach out
For a steadying hand

I can't cope with questions
I need a strong and slow voice
To talk to me about anything
Anything that I can cling to
Anything that will help me focus

Not everyone understands my plight
I know their frustration
But that just makes me worse
How can they know blind terror
If I can't explain

Shelter From the Storm

For years I thought you were the enemy
But now I know you are my friend
You are instantly here for me
Even before I realise I need you
And you never fail me

As an impenetrable shield
You separate me from a reality
Too big for my mind to grasp the edges of
Giving me time to adjust
To some inescapable horror

I know you are only temporary
But that's fine with me
You don't block out the beautiful
Though the sun isn't as bright
And nothing tastes or smells the same

You let me test myself
By opening a small window
Is the monster still there?
Yes!   I slam the window shut
And wait for another day

Cautiously I try again
Hold my breath and wait
It appears to be safe
The monster has shrunk
To a manageable reality

Shock, my friend, when you recede
I don't miss you
You are a constant in my life
I just rejoice that I don't have to fear
Getting hopelessly lost

Wordsmiths Silenced

We were thrust
Into this alien world
Of procedures and routines
Like frightened children
At an unknown railway station

Surgery left you deprived
Of the power of speech
And for a few days
You had to use pen and paper
To answer endless questions

But this was of little help
In the long and lonely nights
When you felt as if you were choking
And pressing the bell
Didn't bring assistance quickly enough

Exhaustion took its toll
And robbed me of solid reason
I was rendered speechless
By too many things
I was struggling to take in

I shuddered, stuttered and sobbed
Shook my head in denial
As if to shake the words loose
Fighting terror and panic
That I would not regain coherence

What use all those words
That we use to weave this
Magic carpet of our lives
When we cannot use our voices
And must rely on touch?

Aftermath

I wrote once about
The aftermath of a bushfire
And how the sweet blessing
Of rain falling cleansed
The earth for new growth

How well I know
The relief and healing
Of shuddering sobs
And tears that fall
As if without end

I hope there will be
No end to the tears
I have fought bitterness
Too hard for too long
To let it win now

Tears from the heart
Can only do good
It is sad that some
Seek only to stem the flow
Because they feel uncomfortable

Cancer

The woman, the lover, the poet
All are being undone by this word
It is the echoes of other people's experiences
That are making me unwilling to examine
What I really think and feel

Horror stories come thick and fast
Both of my grandfathers
And my own father
Died because of cancer
But I was too far away to be a witness

Many times I have heard
Of heroic battles to overcome cancer
With surgery, radiotherapy and chemotherapy
Till the spring of life is eventually broken
But who tells of the quality of life won?

Of the deep joy and satisfaction
Felt by a mother or father
As they live long enough
To watch their children grow
While grieving for what they will miss

Clever words and good ones
But still the poet is on the run
I dare you to say it out loud
What if they don't destroy it?
What if it comes back bigger and better?

I learned the hard way
There is no trading with death
Is trading with life any different?
Better to say 'fuck it'
And live each day to the fullest

Dark Shadow

What exquisite sensations
Through heart, body, mind and spirit
To know the trauma and indignities
Were not in vain
That the bone is clear of cancer

Still a rough road to be walked
The precautionary radiotherapy
Would like to threaten our peace
But you – the uninvited, unwelcome guest
No longer have the prime place in our lives

What a dark and terrifying shadow
You have cast
I have experienced fear in many ways
But nothing like you with your
Brooding presence waiting to pounce

Keeping us taught inside
As if we have been held together by
Overstretched elastic and rusty paper clips
Daring ourselves to feel the joy
But always something held in reserve

We are not so arrogant
That we can cast care to the wind
No doubt your echoes will haunt us
But now you are just another name
For the darkness that makes the light so good

Going Home

How hard Stephen worked
To bring this day forward
As much as possible
Never mind the hospital's edict
Of fourteen days

He was a compliant patient
He did everything they asked
Watched the boxes being ticked
That meant he would be released
And on the twelfth day it was so

But what unexpected fears there were
Donning outdoor clothing
Wielding his walking stick
Facing the open world
With all its buffeting

Like it or not
We had become accustomed
To the regularity of hospital routine
Having so little control
Over anything that happened

We almost escaped unnoticed
But were apprehended at the last post
A nurse was supposed to have
Escorted us safely off the premises
Still more checks for boxes to be ticked

But at last we made it
Together we ran the gauntlet
Of smokers and visitors
That constantly adorn
The front entrance of the hospital

We stepped into a taxi
Sat back and let ourselves be driven
Only sighing with relief
When we stepped through the garden gate
And heard the satisfying click as it locked behind us

Reprieve

Oh such bliss to be home
To potter gently around
The house and the garden
Go into the office and check
What needed to be done

To sleep in his own bed
Perhaps not as peacefully
As he would have liked
But far more comfortable
Than the one he had known

To sit out on the balcony
With a glass of wine
And soak in the healing
Of fresh breezes and sunlight
On his face and watch dolphins

Eating real food
Such delight at home cooking
Hours spent talking with his daughter
As she helped make up back orders
Making him laugh

Evenings playing Scrabble
Two minds so alike and so competitive
But underneath a deep love
Emerging to depose
Any long-ago hostility

This was a reprieve
A few days to catch our breath
Before Karyn had to return to England
And the radiotherapy treatment
Was due to begin

Celebration Bash

Some instinct for survival
Made me suggest
We have a bash to celebrate
Several auspicious events
As a reminder of good fortune

I wanted the comfort
Of friends and family
I needed them to see for themselves
That Stephen had come through
And he was all right

We all needed to believe
Things would go back to normal
And these loved ones have now seen
That we are not the same
And we are learning a new normal

Going On

It has been so lovely
Having Karyn here
Her cheerful bravery
Keeping at bay
The fears and doubts

But today she is flying
Back to wintry England
And our hearts ache
That she cannot stay here
A talisman against the dark

We sit on the veranda
Eating ham sandwiches
Drinking a glass of wine
Watching sparrows squabble
Over who gets to eat the bread crumbs

The rose bush stands quietly
Pretty pink blossoms
Nod lazily in the sun
Everything is warm and peaceful
And serenity finds a way in

We have our own strength
We each learned it for ourselves
And there is no shadow of doubt
That we can do what we have to do
With dignity and honour

Trust

The next stage has started
It all sounds so simple
Targeting an area from
Five different directions
And it won't hurt at all

Except what will happen
To his poor face
And the inside of his mouth?
And how to keep up protein intake
And deal with accumulating tiredness

We have an appointment schedule
That takes us through thirty treatments
The staff are so caring and compassionate
The waiting area even has jigsaw puzzles
Why then am I still so frightened?

Because like so often before
In this lifetime
I have had to make
A conscious decision
To trust someone to do it right

And doctors are only people
They have frailties
Just like the rest of us
Yet they have chosen a profession
Bearing great responsibility

It is for me to remember this
And allow that they will
Do everything they can
To destroy any trace of the cancer
That insinuated itself into our lives

Return Visits

It's the first day of a complete week
Last week was like a trial run
With getting parking permits sorted
Establishing the best route to and fro
Getting accustomed to trepidation

Over the weekend I reminded myself
Who I am, not the faded person
I was in danger of becoming
Unable to trust my own strength
Whose self-confidence was wavering

It is not easy coming here
Much like bringing the children
To doctor and dentist appointments
Having to be calm and brave
Re-assuring and comforting

It is far worse for him
He is the one they strap down
With his custom-made mask
Holding his poor face still
As they bombard it with rays

It will be during this week
The effects will make themselves known
His face will turn red and sore
We aren't sure about inside his mouth
And the dreaded tiredness

I wonder why this part frightens me so
Perhaps because I don't want to see him
Become disabled by weakness
That even his determination
Will be seriously challenged by

I must be careful
In the times ahead
Not to be impatient
With those who do not come with us
On this daily trek

Those who will not see first hand
The changes that will occur
Those who hide behind
Busy nothing rather than
Offer to be part of the process of healing

Paradox

Yesterday I was cross
At this ponderous mechanism
That dictates the shape of our days
Telling us when we have to report
How long we must be here

It is a paradox that
This regime is saving his life
Giving us a future
Yet impinging on our lives
As if as individuals we count for nothing

The staff do so much
To help stop it all becoming
Too impersonal
With gentle humour
Brief exchanges when they can

But they don't know us
They have no idea what enriches us
What music we like
What books we read, movies we watch
Who our friends are

It is all about balance again
Different realities
Each equally real and important
A tenuous temporary link
Made out of grim necessity

Five Minutes a Day

I might be sitting
In the waiting-room
Of the radiotherapy suite
While Stephen has his treatment
But this five minutes is mine alone

Hard to block out rubbish television
The constant hum of the air-conditioner
Somehow I need to look inside
Remind myself that I am a person
And I have a right to my life

Instead of writing another poem
I shall imagine painting a picture
Getting lost in creating
Long-stemmed poppies and wheat
Against a clear blue sky

I want to be part of the simplicity
And forget the complications
Of trying to keep the peace
Making other people feel comfortable
For five minutes I don't have to care

Not Vanity

Modern technology is brilliant
Skilled doctors are equally so
Nurses help weave it all together
A battle plan is drawn up and executed
A life is given another chance

There is much to be thankful for
Life, sweet life
More days to see the sun
More nights to wonder at
More opportunities to be with those we love

But there has been such a high price to pay
Dignity, self-esteem, even the will to live
Have been battered beyond belief
Making a sensitive person
Want to hide in the dark like a wounded animal

It is hard enough growing older
Watching our hair turn grey
Our skin becoming wrinkled
Physical strength wane
Without the gross intrusion of surgery

It isn't some egocentric vanity
To grieve over the loss of a seen identity
We all have an image of ourselves
How we want to be
How we hope other people see us

Delusion of Next Door

We have become familiar
With the maze of roads
Within the hospital grounds
And with some smugness
Cruise to the 'permit holders only' area

We walk behind the radiotherapy building
Pretending we don't care
Are no longer worried
About the reason we are here
Deluding no one – especially not us

As we come around the corner
Past a tall trellis covered in white stars
The air is filled with sweet perfume
And for a few minutes we are transported
To the Botanic Gardens next door

Reminder

It's day eleven of thirty
The side-effects
Are beginning to be felt
And we were feeling glum
At the prospect of the road ahead

We told the receptionist
We were tired of this game
She said she would change the rules
And there was such understanding
In the steady gaze that met mine

We all knew it was a nonsense
But it's these quips that help a lot
Then a wheelchair was pushed past us
With a young person in it
Whose bald pate told it's own story

The doctor's words echoed
'Cancer is indiscriminate'
I thought, awful as it is for us
How much worse for a youngster
Just starting on their journey of life

What of parents and siblings?
I worked with a woman
Who was struck with helpless outrage
Devastated when her small granddaughter
Was diagnosed with leukaemia

After a few years in remission
The cancer is back and will stay
It was an important reminder of our good fortune
Stephens cancer was surgically removed
The radiotherapy just a precaution

Time Out

Yesterday was hot and humid
The blue sky was blanketed
In dense grey clouds
Beautifully designed
And interlaced

The rain came by lunchtime
Lovely steady rain
That the thirsty earth
Soaked up, flowers absorbed
And the roads and paths were washed clean

I dead-headed the roses in the garden
How pungent it all smelled
Petals falling, sticking to my fingers
The lavender bush needs to be moved
To where the erica has crisped up and died

This morning we drove to the hospital early
The roads through the parklands
Almost empty of cars
The trees are heavy with raindrops
And are richly green

I've always liked the early morning city
Before the cars fill the air with fumes
When the sound of birds can be heard
The river looks as if it's still sleeping
With the occasional eager rower stretching

The great mechanism of the hospital
Is grinding into action
Cars are queuing for parking spaces
Staff are hurrying to start their shifts
There is the constant hum of generators

Life

What is it that drives us
What is this life
What mystery is this
That we cling to
With such tenacity?

The waiting room
Is a place of positive vibrations
Not just from caring staff
But every person I see there
Undergoing treatment

They don't appear to be wasting energy
Raving about the why of any of it
They are focused on getting better
What hidden dreams they must have
What goals yet unattained

Another Reality

We went for a walk
Amid majestic trees
Graceful statuary
Early morning peace
In the Botanic Gardens

For a few minutes
It was a different world
I wasn't pretending
It was real
The sense of wholeness

I wonder how much
Was due to the trees
I felt again their embrace
Their strength   their patience
Anchoring me to the earth

Half-kisses

You worry about eating
Or drinking a cup of coffee
When foodstuffs drip
Onto your chin
And you don't feel them

You were concerned
That you could not smile
That your mouth would droop
That people would stare
And possibly pity

Because since forever
Some of the hallmarks
Of being an imbecile
Have been those
Physical manifestations

For me I notice
That your kisses are different
One of your half-kisses
Is worth more
Than any amount of 'sucking face'

In Awe

The nurse calls his name
Her voice is warm
And full of caring
When she asks the inevitable
'How are you today?'

And he answers
In a strong voice
As he strides to meet her
That he is doing all right
This makes me weep

I am in awe
Of his courage and fortitude
His ability to be calm
When all I want to do
Is run and run and run

Dungeon

I don't know why
I can't seem to bring
The outdoors into
This dungeon of a
Waiting room

There are no windows
No breath of fresh air
The leaf-sprigged carpet
A mockery
Of a forest floor

The TV is never turned off
And even the cheerful staff
Can't change the fact
We are separate
From the other real world

Of sunshine and rain showers
Gleaming wet roads
The delicate call
Of birds in the trees
The hustle and bustle of life

Tree Help

More and more
I am reaching out
To the trees
As we drive to the hospital
For the early appointments

I feel them closing around me
Giant sentinels
Sparkling with dew
Or overnight rain
Another steadying hand

Would that I could
Sit beneath one
Lean my back against the trunk
Feel the sap running
Slow and sure

Slowing my mind
That is racing
Like a panic-stricken animal
Not as jumpy as before
But not at ease

My prayers in the shower
Help me start the day
And the days are
Inexorably passing
I see them being ticked off

But I still seem detached
From myself
Wanting to fight
But no enemy is forthcoming
Except the sense of helplessness

Metallica

It is the nature of the man
That he does not complain
And I slipped into
A false sense of security
That the effects weren't getting worse

He mentioned near the beginning
That his food tasted differently
So I shouldn't have been
So surprised today when he quipped
About his breakfast

The hated chemical compound
That he so reluctantly ingests
Pureed fruit a cup of coffee
Then he added about the
Extra taste of metal

He reminded me
He had been told
This would happen
It was I
Who had forgotten

No Claustrophobia Today

I promised myself
I wouldn't let claustrophobia
Get me today
After all I'm not the one
Having to wear the mask

I said I would bring
the sunshine in with me
And low and behold
It has worked
Better than I imagined

Mind you, it helps
That the TV is on so quiet
I can barely hear it
And the book I brought in to read
Is beautifully descriptive of outdoors

Natural Remedies

Being surrounded by technology
It is good to be reminded
Of nature's remedies
That dispel gloom
And uplift the senses

War Memorial Drive winds its way
Between the golf course
And the slow moving river
The traffic was paused
For a majestic black swan

An unusual call caught my attention
As we sat at the traffic lights
A trio of black cockatoos
Flew from one tree to another
They were a long way from home

A pair of ghost egrets
Pace gracefully in the shallows
They are like mirrored images
Snowy white necks outstretched
In search of lunch

The dolphin adults
Are teaching the baby to fish
By smacking its tail on the water
The sound is so loud
It can wake us from sleeping

W.H. Davies had it right
In his poem titled 'Leisure'
'What is this life,
If full of care
We have no time to stand and stare…'

Identification

I remember when some years ago
I had to have a hysterectomy
I felt overnight I had become ordinary
The same as so many other women
Whose lives had been dealt this card

I was a reluctant member
Of a sisterhood I had long shunned
I had set myself apart
Glorying in the pleasure
Of being an individual

But the damage was done
The surgeon's knife carved away
Cleanly, it must be said,
The very heart of how I identified myself
How I was with others

And Stephen too has striven
To be an individual man
Not allowed himself
To be dictated to
In order to fit in

I worked hard to ensure
Friends and family knew
This whole experience
Was all about Stephen
That his needs would come first

How much will his identity
Be affected now he is one
Of a celebrated band of brothers
Who have faced the terror of cancer
And lived to tell the tale?

A Little Harmless Deception

We have been counting
Off the days
Finding a landmark
In a fraction gained
Only a fraction to go

Past the halfway mark
Downhill now
The next goal to be reached
A single-number day
Later this week

I thought how quickly
The days have gone
How soon it will be over
Well, this stage
Of the process anyway

But you silently shook your head
Reminding me
Of the endless times
You have had to lie
Trapped within the mask

How little I know
Of your journey
How I have underestimated
The source of strength
We are for each other

Only Lunch

We sat down to lunch
As we have so many times before
But my attention was drawn
To the differences
In the food before us

You from necessity
Have a bowl of soup
Not even homemade today
With a flavour barely discernible
Except for the metallic aftertaste

I have a plate of green –
Lettuce   celery   cucumber –
Pieces of cheese
And to add insult to injury
Salt and vinegar chips

A different person
Would have had
The same as you
As a show of support
Of solidarity in suffering

But I am me
And I needed crunchy green
Just as I need to swim in the sea
Or go out on my bike
Before we share our singular breakfasts

Time Passing

It is not cowardice
That finds me in this garden
A place of seclusion
While Stephen has his treatment
In suite five today not suite two

How I despise the television
With the American voices
Whining and nasal
Stirring their mixing bowl
Of shallow dramas

But more disturbing
How sorrowful are they
Who sit attention glued to the screen
Can that really be better
Than their own reality?

I've vowed and boasted
I wouldn't wish time away
But it is hard these days
To stop thinking
'Let's get another treatment over'

I find a goal in each new week
Something to look forward to
Today there is only one more Wednesday
Tomorrow there are only
Single-number days to go

Walk a Mile In His Shoes

I walked with him into the treatment room
Watched as he climbed on the bed
And the delightful girls set the mask in place
Anchoring him with no ability to move
Even his eyes are forced closed

We all stepped out into another room
The therapists checked their numbers
So vigilant so precise
They answered my questions about
Who decided on the dosage needed

Explained about the five beams
Each having its individual turn
To bombard a specific area
I watched intrigued the screens
Of four computers

But that was early on in the piece
Then I was afraid to climb inside
His head and heart
Afraid to try and imagine
How he might be feeling

Day twenty of thirty treatments
He had to go to another suite
I asked if it made any difference
He said 'It still burned the hell out of me
And made more ulcers'

Courage Is Hard To Measure

Do I lack courage
Because I don't always ask
How he is each morning
Or if he is all right
Before or after the treatments

This morning his quick wit
Made me quip back
'Did you have razor blades for supper?'
He said 'Every meal
Is like eating razor blades'

While Stephen was in hospital
A visiting writer
Sent me an encouraging email
He referred to Stephen
Having the stoic look

How right he was
Neither of us lack courage
But we do have
Our individual ways
Of walking this path

Passionate Alternative

For the self-indulgent person
It is easy to let emotions
Run their full length and depth
And no one thinks it amiss
If they give vent to frustration and pain

The drunk gets hammered
And becomes violent or maudlin
Breaking treasures indiscriminately
Hurling abuse at the innocent
Then crying remorsefully into their glass

For the one who has the gift of words
Writing down thoughts and feelings
Releases the pain and gives others
The opportunity to know
That none of us are alone

For the musician his pain
Becomes exquisite harmonies
Sending perfection
Into the far reaches of the ether
Bringing solace to all who can hear

For the quiet one
Whose thoughts fly higher and wider
Feelings go deeper and broader
Than the average person
There is no such freedom

Their silence thrums with a different intensity
They withdraw from the shallow
And remain the steadying hand
Doing what must be done without complaint
But sometimes there is a wistful look

No More Questions

I decided there was no point
In asking any more questions
Because the answers were all the same
And 'I don't know'
Doesn't cut it any more

I had wondered what would happen
If Stephen's skin cracked
Under the onslaught of rays
Would there be an interruption
To the procedure

But no, they keep going
Just offering a different cream
And painkillers
That don't appear to bring
The promised relief

The doctor knows I have changed
She knows she has lost me
As her ally
She is on her own now
If she wants Stephen to believe something

She doesn't know how to deal
With Stephen's stoicism
It would be easier for her
If he ranted and raved
About the unfairness of it all

Then she could trot out
Her set pieces about difficulties
The unknowns of her profession
How lucky we are
With the successes

Necessity

There have been times in this life
When I have been called upon
To trust someone with me
And I have made the conscious decision
To allow myself to be vulnerable

I have been prepared
To accept and live with
The consequences of my choice
My heart has been broken
My spirit bowed

There have been times
When I have had to trust
Someone not for love
But for their skill and expertise
To fix what I am unable to

But I don't trust them at all
They are not gods with their knowledge
They are not invincible
They are just people like me
With frailties and flaws

Who do their best
To instil confidence
In those who sit before them
With silent pleading in their eyes
Like children being offered for sacrifice

They do not blatantly lie
They don't promise the perfect cure
They carefully lace their language
With words like 'might' and 'wait'
Then watch as hope dies

Almost Done

At last I have stopped being angry
I have been so hurt
That no one offered
To be part of this imposed routine
And know first-hand what it has been like

I won't miss these trips
Though I always enjoy
Going anywhere with Stephen
And as usual we have
Made our own fun

For the past couple of weeks
We have been counting
The cars displaying antlers
Unsure who is the silliest
Us or the owners

Our lives are richer
For this shared experience
Once again I know
What I will do for love
And that is a good feeling

These are days to rejoice
Only four more treatments
How keenly we count them
A touch of hysteria?
Quite likely and why not!

We always knew
We would come through intact
Could it have been made easier?
I am like the doctors
I don't know

Old Tricks

We have been steadily
Ticking off the days
Almost there
Only three more
Treatments to go

We accepted with a shrug
The doctor telling us last week
The symptoms would keep
Getting worse for a week
After the last one

I went on alert mode on Monday
When the doctor
Said 'Don't cancel the dietician
If you need her in two or three weeks
It will be hard to get you in'

Not so easy to dismiss when
This morning one of the technicians
Said the symptoms
Will keep getting worse
For up to a month

We teased ourselves
With the idea of asking the doctor
At our last appointment next Monday
Maybe it will be six weeks
But they won't know and might not see the joke

Ducks and Swans

Nature has rescued me again
Down by the river
A pair of black swans
Surrounded by their
Half grown cygnets

The curve of their necks
So haughty and grand
They deigned to permit
Some intrusive photographer
To do what he thought he had a right to

Another morning it was ducks
Mum and dad herding
About a dozen little fluff balls
Safely across the road
And down to the water

Quite rightly the traffic stopped
To allow this procession
Free passage
After all it is their world
Not just ours

Bereft

Our lives have been caught up
With the hospital schedule
Living day to day
Varying our activities
Around the appointment times

I haven't given much thought
To whether the treatment is working
I don't lack courage
But it seems a pointless exercise
Speculating about the unknown

But soon we will be cast loose
Only two more treatments
Then we are on our own again
Without the ponderous presence
Of the hospital system

There is trepidation in my heart
I have become so used
To having our lives dictated to
By dietary needs, treatments
Keeping up a brave face

I don't feel so brave today
It has been a long journey
And I am bone weary
Of pretending to be all right
That my senses aren't being battered

Instead of rejoicing
I feel grief-stricken
In the weeks ahead
We must forge a new normal
Which will have some of the old

Last Day

The last day did come
The receptionist gave me such a warm hug
I think she has a good idea
How much she helped me
Through the relentless days

The nurse cheerfully
Loaded us up with supplies
The mouthwashes that spoil
The lingering hint of a taste of food
The cream for his face

The therapists so excited
That this was the last treatment
When it was all done
They gave Stephen his mask
A funny kind of trophy

We walked along the corridor
Towards the sunlight streaming through the door
I noticed that the flowers on the trellis
Were all gone – along with their perfume
We got in the car and drove home

Living

The Muse has chosen me
And I have written many poems
Over these past weeks
A journal with a difference
About thoughts and feelings

There are those who frown
Sometimes in anger and frustration
Sometimes in sadness
That I allow myself to go down
With the weight of grief

Kind hearts have gifted me
Poetry, songs, stories
Meant to guide me away
From the sorrows that are mine
And bring me back to the light

And I know my own frustration
That no one seems to understand
That it is all part of feeling alive
Just as laughing in the waves
Of an ocean swept by storms

Laughter or tears
What does it matter
My body feels alive
I feel the blood in my veins
The swelling in my heart

Such are the joys I know
They fly me to the heights
It is only nature's law of balance
That there must be the depths
To which I can plunge and emerge victorious

The Outer Edge

I feel like someone has had me
At the end of a long rope
And it delighted them to
Swing the rope and me around
Like an Olympian twirling a hammer throw

All energy was concentrated
On establishing the right momentum
Calculating in the relevant forces
Making exacting demands for accuracy
Factoring in resources

It wasn't me anchored to the ground
I was too busy swirling
Desperately trying to identify familiar landmarks
Grasping onto those who beyond all logic
Gave me some semblance of steadiness

Now the unseen hand has set me free
No longer twirling and swirling
I have been granted a new perspective
Where the core of me is stronger
And the dross has been flung to the outer edge

www.ingramcontent.com/pod-product-compliance
Lightning Source LLC
Chambersburg PA
CBHW062140100526
44589CB00014B/1640